NEW WAYS FOR FAMILIES®

COLLABORATIVE PARENT WORKBOOK

I0805689

UNHOOKED BOOKS
AN IMPRINT OF HIGH CONFLICT INSTITUTE PRESS
SCOTTSDALE ARIZONA USA

Third edition.

A Note to the Reader

This publication is designed to provide accurate and authoritative information about the subject matters covered. It is sold with the understanding that neither the author nor publisher are rendering legal, mental health, medical or other professional services, either directly or indirectly. If expert assistance, legal services or counseling is needed, the services of a competent professional should be sought. Names and identifying information of private individuals have been changed to preserve anonymity. Neither the authors nor the publisher shall be liable or responsible for any loss or damage allegedly arising as a consequence of your use or application of any information or suggestions in this book.

ISBN-13: 978-1936268061

Publisher
Unhooked Books
7701 E. Indian School Rd., Ste. F
Scottsdale, AZ 85251 USA
www.unhookedbooks.com

Ordering and Contact Information
High Conflict Institute®/New Ways for Families®
Email: info@newways4families.com
Website: NewWays4Families.com

Printed in the United States of America

Contents

Part I: New Ways for Families®
Parent Coaching Sessions

Introduction

New Ways for Families is a new method for parents to help themselves and their children through a divorce or separation, without becoming stuck in conflict.

Approximately 25% of divorcing parents (including unmarried parents), remain in "high conflict" more than two years after they separate. They have three key negative habits that keep them stuck, which are predictable and generally become worse during the divorce process: *all-or-nothing thinking, unmanaged emotions, and extreme behaviors.* These habits spill over onto their children and push their children away from one or both parents, causing the children long-term health and mental health problems, as indicated by recent studies.

New Ways for Families was designed to prevent or reduce the use of these three habits as soon as possible, and to lay the groundwork for using three conflict-reducing skills instead, throughout the separation and divorce process:

Flexible Thinking

Managed Emotions

Moderate Behaviors

This Workbook contains short articles and exercises to help you strengthen these skills so that you can use them in communicating with the other parent, in making decisions, and in helping your child or children handle the separation or divorce process with resilience. This Workbook should be discussed with your Coach as early in the Collaborative process as possible, although it can be used at any time. Then, after three meetings with your Coach(es), this Workbook provides a structure for meeting with your children and your Collaborative Child Specialist.

Both Parents
By having both parents practice the same skills, it should help both of you in your communications, making proposals, making decisions and parenting. It will also help avoid endless battles over the past and who is to blame for this or that. At the same time, important problems can be addressed, if needed, in a problem-solving manner. It helps you avoid over-reacting to statements or behavior of the other parent, while setting limits where necessary. New Ways is about finding balance and keeping the focus on what to do now.

Future Focus
New Ways focuses on skills to use for the future. During a separation or divorce, it is easy to become overwhelmed, sad or angry in thinking about the past. If feelings are too intense during this time, counseling is recommended outside of the Collaborative process. In New Ways, the focus is on skills to help you communicate respectfully and successfully with each other; skills to help you negotiate by making proposals; skills to help you make

decisions, now and in the future; and skills to help you work together in parenting your children.

Practice
All of these skills take practice and are often the *opposite of what you feel like doing!* So it helps for each of you to be using the same skills and for the professionals working with you in Collaborative Divorce to also be using and encouraging the use of the same skills. You already know and use these basic skills in other areas of your life, and during simpler times. The importance of practice is so that you can automatically use these skills *even when* you are upset and *even when* you have big decisions to make.

Structure of this Method
New Ways for Families® in Collaborative Divorce is structured to focus on skills first, then on decisions. Therefore, it is designed as follows:

With Coach(es):

1. Two separate New Ways meetings with each parent and Coach
2. One joint New Ways meeting with both parents and Coach(es)

With Child Specialist:

3. Two separate New Ways meetings with each parent, children and Child Specialist
4. One or more joint New Ways meeting with both parents, children and Child Specialist

Flexibility
This method is designed to be flexible, so that parents, coaches and/or child specialists can meet more often than the sessions described above, and can add issues for discussion in separate or joint meetings. Essentially, you should collaborate in making any changes to this basic method, so that it works most effectively for you. However, it has been designed based on the author's many years of studying what doesn't work. So you are encouraged to use this process without reducing the number of meetings or exercises – just add to it when agreed upon by those involved.

Not Therapy
Collaborative Coaches and Child Specialists are not acting as therapists. Therefore, New Ways for Families® in Collaborative Divorce is not designed to be therapy. If you wish to have some therapy, you should meet with an outside therapist who uses the New Ways for Families® method in therapy (there are different workbooks for that) – or other therapy methods.

The benefit of an outside therapist is that you can continue in therapy after the divorce decisions have been made. Coaches and Child Specialists in Collaborative Divorce focus on making decisions and their work is done once the decisions have been made. Therefore, it is important that you, your coach and child specialist do not attempt to open up deep emotional issues or "family-of-origin" issues while learning the New Ways skills and making the decisions described in New Ways.

On the other hand, your experience in the collaborative process may help you decide that you want to see a therapist in the future after the divorce decisions have been made. This can be very helpful in changing some personal habits and in making future relationship decisions. Your coach cannot be your future therapist, although he or she may be able to recommend one.

Using This Workbook with Your Coach
This Workbook is designed to provide information, topics for discussion and exercises to practice the skills. Both parents are expected to work on the same skills and the same exercises in their own Workbooks. Ideally, you will be working on these at the same time, so that you will be ready to meet with your Child Specialist to use these skills with your children at the same time.

1. **First New Ways Coaching Meeting**
   Bring your workbook to your first coaching meeting about New Ways for Families®. If possible, read the Skills and Articles before that first meeting. You will discuss them in your meeting.

2. **Before Your Second New Ways Coaching Meeting**
   Write the exercises as much as possible. Just do the best you can.

3. **Second New Ways Coaching Meeting**
   Discuss the written exercises, then write statements that apply to your own decisions or issues in regard to the other parent and your children. For example, if the other parent writes hostile emails, write a practice response to a hostile email based on the skills in the article "Responding to Hostile Email (B.I.F.F.)." Prepare for your third New Ways Coaching Meeting which will be a joint meeting with the other parent. Discuss with your coach how you can use these skills to make that meeting most successful and lay the groundwork for a future collaboration as parents.

4. **Before Your Third New Ways Coaching Meeting**
   Write the positive statements, requests and proposals described in the Workbook, which you would like to present at this joint meeting.

5. **Third New Ways Coaching Meeting (Joint)**
   Present your statements, requests and proposals and listen to the other parent's statements, requests and proposals (while practicing your skills). Follow your coach(es) directions in making this a successful meeting.

If you have any further questions about this method, contact your coach.

Best Wishes!

Session 1: Three Skills for Resilience

Separation and divorce can be one of the most difficult times in your life, and in your children's lives. However, decades of research has shown that the *way* you handle the separation or divorce can make a world of difference. Also, we live in times of great change in many areas of our lives, so that skills for resilience can help you and your children in all aspects of your life.

When a parent gets stuck in conflict, it's usually because they didn't use these three skills:

Flexible Thinking

Managed Emotions

Moderate Behaviors

Then, the other parent reacts and doesn't use these skills either.

You might know these skills and use them in other situations, but in the tension and uncertainty of separation and divorce, any normal human being can forget. Therefore, this workbook and method is designed to help *both* parents practice these skills enough so that they do not forget when it really matters: in communicating with the other parent, in making decisions and in communicating with your children.

Examples of what parents do instead include the following:

All-or-nothing thinking (seeing yourself as perfect, wishing other parent was dead, etc.)

Unmanaged emotions (frequent yelling, blaming, crying in front of the children, etc.)

Extreme behaviors (domestic violence, child abuse, child alienation, false reports, etc.)

In many "high-conflict" families, only one parent has these characteristics and the other parent is trying hard to be reasonable and protect the children. In other high conflict families, both parents have some of these characteristics, although one may be more extreme than the other.

Therefore, so that you do not become a high-conflict parent, and to encourage the other parent, practicing the positive skills in this workbook can make a real difference. Research also shows that children exposed to their parents' anger, fear and conflict can be harmful to their long-term health and mental health. So the more you are both able to manage your own skills, even under stress, the better off your children will be. Then, you can also teach your children these skills to help them be resilient through your divorce.

Personal Goals

In order to practice and remember these skills under stress, it helps to think of some goals that you have for yourself regarding these three skills. Think about which of the following might apply to you:

> "To practice flexible thinking when my partner/spouse is blaming me for everything."

"To manage my emotions when the children criticize my actions."
"To respond with moderate behaviors when my partner/spouse sends angry emails."
"To get my partner/spouse to listen to me when I make parenting suggestions."
"To protect my children from the other parent's negative comments and behavior."
"To learn ways to calm myself down when I am upset around the children."

Think of some other goals you might have which would be helped by using flexible thinking, managed emotions, and moderate behaviors. As you go through the process of communicating with the other parent, making decisions and communicating with your children, "check yourself" to see of you are practicing these skills and if they are helping you. And remind yourself: no one's perfect! (That's flexible thinking!)

Think of one goal you have for yourself regarding *flexible thinking, managed emotions,* or *moderate behavior,* during your separation or divorce, and write it here:

Exercise #1:

My personal goal: ____

____

Hurdles

Speaking of not being perfect, there are various hurdles that you should expect may come up while you are trying to maintain *flexible thinking, managed emotions, and moderate behaviors.* If you can, think ahead now of what some of these might be. Then, think of how you might deal with them. Here's some examples. See if any of these fit you. If not, see if you can think of some that might – and how you could deal with them when they arise.

Examples:

HURDLES TO NEW WAYS FOR FAMILIES	WAYS OF DEALING WITH THEM
I don't want to do this New Ways stuff.	I don't have to like it. I can just do it. I might learn something anyway.
When I get upset, it's hard to calm down.	I can practice the suggestions in this workbook.
I'm a perfectionist and I'm afraid I won't do the exercises right.	There's no "right way" in New Ways for Families. All you have to do is practice and write about flexible thinking, managing emotions, and using moderate behaviors in response to difficult situations.
I don't want this divorce, so I don't want to learn skills to help it happen.	These are useful skills and may help me improve this relationship or future ones.
The other parent pushes my buttons all the time.	I may learn more about new ways to stay cool in the face of the other parent's comments and actions.

Remember Your Strengths

Separation or divorce can make you forget about your strengths, so that it's easy to feel that your "buttons" are being pushed. Take a couple minutes to think about some of your strengths and positive qualities. Reminding yourself of these may help you stay calm and realize that you don't need to defend yourself just because others are upset right now. People can say anything when they're upset, and it's not about you – it's about them. This will help you use *flexible thinking, managed emotions,* and *moderate behaviors.*

Session 1: Flexible Thinking

We are constantly facing new situations that may have never occurred in our lives before, or even in the world before. What we need is flexible thinking for new ways of solving problems in new situations. Flexible thinking means that you will consider several solutions or options for solving a problem. Flexible thinking means that you recognize there are gray areas in most situations.

On the other hand, there is all-or-nothing thinking. It's one of the biggest barriers to success in a changing world. All-or-nothing thinking keeps us stuck in old ways, while flexible thinking helps us keep thinking of new ideas and trying them out until something works.

Here are some common examples of all-or-nothing thinking in separation or divorce:

> "The divorce is all the other parent's fault. There is nothing I need to do differently."
>
> "The divorce is all my fault. I might as well give up trying to have a relationship."
>
> "Everyone is against me. There's nothing I can do."
>
> "Everyone will see things my way. I can't wait to tell them."
>
> "I have to have 50-50 custody. There's nothing to discuss."
>
> "I have to have full custody. There's nothing to discuss."
>
> "Our child doesn't want to see you, and I won't force her."
>
> "It's my pension and you're not getting a penny of it."

Flexible Statements

Which of the following examples do you think shows flexible thinking?

> "I can learn new ways of doing things, regardless of how I did things in the past."
>
> "I prefer to have 50-50 custody, but I'll consider any option that might be good for our kids."
>
> "I must have at least 4 nights a week with the children. That's my line in the sand."
>
> "I've always been the primary parent, but I'm glad the other parent is more involved now."
>
> "The other party wasted money while I saved. I should get 100% of what I saved."
>
> "I worked harder during the marriage, so I should get all of the pension."
>
> "My partner/spouse may be able to change some of his/her parenting behavior. Let's see."

Flexible Thinking in Making Decisions
During separation and divorce, there are many decisions to make, large and small. At times, it will be tempting to slip into rigid, all-or-nothing thinking when making a decision. Therefore, this exercise is to help you practice using flexible thinking, even under stress. Read the article "Yes, No, or I'll Think About It" in Appendix C to this Workbook before this session.

In general, flexible thinking in making proposals and decisions means:

1. There is usually more than one option for solving a problem or planning the future.

2. Explain your reasoning in making your proposals, so that the other person understands your *interests* so that more options can be considered or created that might also fulfill those interests.

3. Seriously consider the other person's proposals before determining whether or not they are realistic.

4. Ask questions to understand the interests or reasoning of the other person's proposals, so that you can consider or create more options that might fit both of your interests.

Exercise #2

Alison and Victor

Alison proposed that Victor pick up the children from her house at 6pm on Fridays on his alternate weekends with the children. She explained that Victor usually worked until 5:30pm every day, so that it would be easy for Victor to pick them up from her house at 6pm.

Victor proposed to pick them up from school at 3pm. He explained that he wanted to be more involved with the children's school now and could change his schedule. He also thought there would be less chance of conflicts between he and Alison if he picked them up at school.

By understanding Victor's reasoning, Alison proposed that he call her the night before if he knew he could get off from work in time to pick them up at school. Otherwise, he could pick them up at her house at 6pm.

Victor liked that general idea because it gave him flexibility with his schedule. But he proposed that he pick them up at school at 3pm unless he calls her the night before and says he can't.

Alison said she would think about his proposal. After a few minutes, she said that it would be impossible for her to plan her Friday afternoons, knowing that he might change his pickup time the night before. Victor said he could respect that concern, so they agreed to start out with the scheduled time of 6pm, unless Victor calls Alison the night before and said he knew he could pick them up at school.

How did Alison and Victor use flexible thinking? Write your thoughts, then discuss with your Coach:

1) ____.

2) ____.

3) ____.

4) ____.

Exercise #3

The House

Pat and Chris are discussing what to do with their house. Pat uses flexible thinking in making some proposals, but Chris does not. How would you suggest that Pat respond to Chris? Write two responses and discuss with your coach.

Pat: I propose that we get an appraisal of the house and see if I can afford to keep the house and buy out your interest somehow.

Chris: That's a ridiculous idea. We have to sell it. We have to put it on the market right away. I refuse to even consider letting you buy me out.

Pat: ____

____

____

Chris: I don't care. I don't like the idea of you living in the house where we lived together.

Pat: ____

____

____

Exercise #4

Your Decision

Write out a proposal for one of your possible decisions and write how you *think* the other person will respond. Then write how you can respond to their response using flexible thinking. Discuss with your coach.

Your Proposal: ____

____

____

____

____

His/Her Response: ____

____

____

____

____

Your Response/New Proposal: ____

____

____

____

____

Discuss with your coach a statement you can practice to remind yourself to use flexible thinking in the future. Write it here. Keep it short and easy to remember.

____

____

If you have time, discuss the following examples with your coach:

A. Joe was 5 minutes late picking up the children for his weekend, so Mary decided that she would leave and take them shopping with her for the next few hours. Was that all-or-nothing thinking? If so, what could Mary have done that shows flexible thinking? What could Joe do that shows flexible thinking?

B. Alicia is not good at math. In discussing their parenting schedule, Robert proposes that she only have parenting time on Saturdays, so that he can help their son with math on weekdays and Sundays. Does his proposal show all-or-nothing thinking? If so, what could Joe do to show flexible thinking? How could Mary respond with flexible thinking?

C. Ellen thinks that the children do not need their father in their life now that they are separated. She and her mother can raise their children just fine without him, she thinks. Is this all-or-nothing thinking? If so, what would be flexible thinking for Ellen?

D. Jack thinks that the children should have no contact with their mother, since she is depressed sometimes and cut her wrists once in a suicide attempt two years ago. Is this all-or-nothing thinking? If so, what would be flexible thinking for Jack?

Session 2: Managed Emotions

As we face new situations in this rapidly changing world, there are many times that we will feel upset. If you are going through a divorce, a job change, a move or any other change, you know what we are talking about. You might feel confused. Or worried. Or angry. Or sad. Yet upset feelings are just feelings and can be managed. Emotions are normal and we all have lots of them.

The goal isn't to eliminate feelings. The goal is to understand what we are feeling and to make decisions about which feelings to act on and which feelings to set aside; which feelings to show and which feelings to hide. Feelings are information which may help us, if we also *think* before we act. But what do we do with the feelings that are *so* upsetting?

Calming Upset Emotions

There are many methods of calming upset emotions.

1. **Take a Break**

One of the most successful ways of calming down is to take a break. This can mean excusing yourself from an angry conversation for a few minutes. "Let me just stop and think for a few minutes." "Let's discuss this later." "I just need some time to think."

Practice saying out loud that you want to take a break.

2. **Talk to someone neutral.**

Separation or divorce are often very upsetting times. When we get upset, it often helps to talk to someone else about it. If possible, it is best to talk to someone who will stay out of the conflict and just lend an ear, so that they don't make things worse for you. Pick someone and call them or visit them and say: "I just need someone to listen for a few minutes. Are you available?"

Think of someone you could call when you are upset.

3. **Tell yourself encouraging statements**

In the Olympics, most of the athletes learn to tell themselves encouraging statements while they are in the middle of extremely difficult challenges—especially when things are going badly and they are feeling very stressed or upset. These statements help them keep their cool.

Think of an encouraging statement you could tell yourself to get through a hard time.

4. **Use flexible thinking to calm your emotions**

Flexible thinking can also help you calm your upset feelings. For example, if you are upset that your child "never listens" to you, think of a time that your child has listened to you. It's not "all or never," although it may feel that way sometimes.

When things go badly, focus on the future and what you can do. Put your energy into flexible thinking to find a good solution if it happens again. For example, if the other parent comes late to pick up the children, think of two or three ways you could deal with that in the future, such as: agreeing that you can leave with the children and arrange a later exchange time; or have a financial penalty for late pickups (like $5 for 15 or more minutes); or changing the next pickup to a later time. Just thinking that you have options can calm you down.

Exercise #5

Practice a situation with your coach in which you might get upset this coming week with a difficult person. First, practice with you being the difficult person saying upsetting things, and let your coach be you, saying what you could say in response. Then, practice with your coach being the difficult person saying upsetting things, and you practice responding.

Write down what you want to remember from this practice exercise, so you can remember to use it this week if the situation comes up.

____

____

If you have time, discuss the following examples with your coach:

A. Mary just found out that Jim is going to be an hour late to pick up the children. She was going to leave to see a movie with a friend after they were picked up, so now she'll miss it. She is very upset. What could she do to calm her upset emotions?

B. Jim feels very controlled by Mary. Now she is on the phone telling him she wants to cancel his parenting time because the children have extra homework tonight that is due tomorrow. He is very upset. How could he tell her he needs to take a break to calm down and think? What could he say to himself before he responds to her? What would be an example of flexible thinking to avoid this in the future?

C. Frank has just threatened over the phone to take Susan back to court to fight for a change of custody, because their daughter is resisting spending time with him this weekend. Susan is very upset to hear this. How could she tell him she needs to take a break to calm down and think? What could she say to herself before she responds to him? What would be an example of flexible thinking to avoid this in the future?

D. Sarah has enrolled their son in soccer in her neighborhood without discussing it with Fred. She just told him as she was dropping off the children. He is furious. What can he do to calm his emotions? What could he say to himself before he responds to her? What would be an example of flexible thinking to avoid this in the future?

Feelings are Contagious

Feelings are contagious. Recent brain research has shown this. If someone is feeling happy, others around him or her will start to feel happier too. If someone is feeling sad, those nearby may also feel sad feelings. Sometimes people pressure us to have the same feeling they are having, especially when they are angry.

Your children may pick up your upset feelings during a separation or divorce. This is very common. It is the same effect when we are at the movies and feel angry or sad along with the main characters. The more attached we are to the character, the more we feel what the character feels. For children, parents are like a movie – as they observe you, they will feel some of what you are feeling.

For example, if you are angry at the other parent in front of your children, they are more likely to become angry at that parent as well. Or if you are sad as they leave to spend time with the other parent, they will feel sad as well. Recent brain research on mirror neurons is starting to explain how this happens. It is usually unconscious and may be unavoidable if children are within sight or hearing of their parents when they are intensely upset.

How can you protect your children from your upset emotions during the separation or divorce process? There are several ways, which especially include keeping your intensely upset emotions about the other parent out of sight and hearing of the children.

A. Out of sight and hearing:

There are many ways you can keep your intense emotions out of sight and hearing of your children. You can go into your room if you are visibly crying or angry. You can talk to a friend in private about how upset you feel, then you will be more able to be calm around your children. If you find that you are crying or angry a lot, you may want to meet with a therapist to get through the upset feelings.

B. Regularly make positive comments:

Regular positive comments about the other parent build resilience against any negative statements and emotions that the children see and hear. Think of three positive qualities of the other parent that you can say regularly to your child/ren:

1. ____

2. ____

3. ____

C. Make "repairing" comments:

Repairing comments are made in any relationship when people say negative things and then say they are sorry and didn't mean to be so negative. For example you could say: "I just said something very negative about your other parent and I didn't mean to be so negative. He/she has many positive qualities and my feelings are my responsibility, not his/hers and not yours. Sorry about that."

Read the article "Is Your Child Alienated?" in Appendix B to this Workbook. It explains more about repairing comments.

Exercise #6

Discuss with your coach a situation that could come up this week in which you could protect your child/ren from your negative emotions about the other parent. Practice what you could say or do with your coach. Write down what you want to remember from this practice exercise, so you can remember to use it this week if the situation comes up.

____

____

MODERATE BEHAVIORS

Extreme behaviors are most often driven by extreme feelings or acting without thinking first. Extreme behaviors include hitting people, hitting children, hiding money, lying, etc. Often people regret using extreme behaviors after their extreme feelings have calmed down. But sometimes people believe that their extreme behaviors were justified because they did what they *felt like doing.*

Feelings aren't Decisions

We are always having feelings. Sometimes they are positive and sometimes they are negative. The goal isn't to eliminate feelings. The goal is to understand what we are feeling and to make decisions about which feelings to act on and which feelings to set aside; which feelings to show and which feelings to hide. Feelings are information which may help us, if we also *think* before we act.

Where do feelings come from? They come from many sources, including (but not limited to):

Our biological needs (hunger, fear of danger, natural drive to be close to people, natural drive to be independent, etc.)

Our life experiences (that certain people are appealing, certain people are dangerous, etc.)

Our self-esteem (how we feel about our appearance, our feelings about money, styles, etc.)

Our moods of the day (hard day at work, child threw up, good friend cheered us up, etc.)

Should you just do it?

Our feelings are significantly influenced by our culture. For example:

> In the 1960's, Janis Joplin said "If it feels good, do it!"
> In the 1970's, Luke Skywalker of Star Wars was told "Go with your feelings!"
> In the 1990's, an advertisement said "Just do it!"
> In the 2000's, an advertisement says "Obey your thirst!"

All of these sayings teach people to act on their feelings without thinking – to act impulsively.

Discuss with your coach whether you think the above sayings are always a good idea, always a bad idea, or sometimes a good idea. Remember flexible thinking.

Think of two situations when you have done what you felt like doing and regretted it afterwards. Discuss with your coach what you learned from those experiences.

Responding to Hostility

Even if you plan to use moderate behaviors, it is often harder to do so when another person is acting in an extreme manner. It is very tempting to respond to extreme behavior with your own extreme behavior. One the of best examples of this today is how people talk to each other on the internet and through email.

Read the article "Responding to Hostile Mail" in Appendix A. Then do the following exercise:

Exercise #7

Eric and Connie

Write a B.I.F.F. response for Eric to Connie based on the email exchange below:

Eric: "I'd like to have Wally on Tuesday evening, June 14th, to attend a father-son baseball game that our group has organized. I know it's usually your night, but I'd like to have this night. I'm willing to switch with another night, in order to be flexible."

Connie: "Eric, you have not been helping Wally enough with his homework on his school nights! I will end your weekday overnights if you don't spend at least two hours helping him study on both of your weekday parenting nights. I want you to keep a record of the exact hours that he spends studying while he is at your house. You know I thought this parenting arrangement wouldn't work out, and it hasn't!!! And you know it!!!"

[Note that she never actually responded to Eric's request. She changed the subject.]

Eric: " ____

____

____

____."

Discuss your response with your coach.

Exercise #8

Erica and Connor

Write a B.I.F.F. response for Erica to Connor based on the email exchange below:

Erica: "I suggest that we get a valuation of your pension, so that we can see if we should divide it, or you could have it all in exchange for another asset of equal value that goes to me. Let me know your thoughts on this. Thanks."

Connor: "That pension is mine and you're not getting a penny of it!! If you go after MY pension, I will force the sale of the house. Then where would you and the kids live? You're a fool if you think that I worked so hard all these years and now I'm going to give you support AND my pension! I will quit my job before I give you a penny of MY pension!!!"

*Erica: "*____

____

____

____."

Discuss your response with your coach.

Exercise #9

Think of a situation in the coming week when you might feel like doing an extreme behavior. Write the situation and a moderate behavior you could use instead:

Situation: ____

____

Moderate behavior: ____

____

Optional Exercise

If you want to, think of two situations where you felt like doing an extreme behavior, but did a moderate behavior instead. Write the behavior you *felt* like doing, then write what you actually did. Then write how you felt about it afterwards: if you were glad or not that you used moderate behavior.

1. What I felt like doing: ______________________________

What I did: ______________________________

How I felt about it afterwards: ______________________________

2. What I felt like doing: ______________________________

What I did: ______________________________

How I felt about it afterwards: ______________________________

Optional Exercise:

Should children just do what they feel?

Discuss with your coach what types of decisions children should make and what types of decisions they shouldn't make. Keep in mind that children are naturally extreme as they try out new behaviors. What they feel like doing is often extreme and not what they need to learn to do, which is moderate behaviors which will help them get along with others throughout their lives. Make a list of each:

DECISIONS CHILDREN SHOULD MAKE	DECISIONS THEY SHOULD NOT MAKE
1. ______________________	1. ______________________
______________________	______________________
2. ______________________	2. ______________________
______________________	______________________
3. ______________________	3. ______________________
______________________	______________________

For the decisions that children should make on the left above, describe the role that feelings should play in making each of those types of decisions. For example, if a child wanted to play on the soccer team, but felt that he or she would be embarrassed, would that be a good reason to decide not to play? For another example, if a teenager felt like kissing a boy or girl, would that be a good reason to just do it?

For the decisions that children should not make on the right above, describe the age at which they should be able to decide these things:

____

____

____

____

Preparing for Joint Session:

New Ways of Making Decisions

Now that you and your partner/spouse are separated or divorced, it will be very important for your children that the two of you make good decisions for them. The next session is a joint meeting with both of you. The session will focus on what your children can learn from each of you and the new ways you want to make decisions in the future for your children's benefit. Make arrangements for the last session.

Exercise #10

Before you meet with your coach(es), think about and write your proposals:

1. How you propose communicating with each other (such as by email, phone, etc.):

   ____

2. The types of decisions that you should make jointly for your child/ren's best interests:

   ____

   ____

   ____

3. The types of decisions that you should make separately for your child/ren:

   ____

   ____

   ____

4. The types of decisions that your child/ren can make:

   ____

   ____

   ____

Preparing for Joint Session:

Learning from Mom, Learning from Dad

To be resilient in today's world, your children need to learn many points of view and many ways of doing things. They need to be able to learn that people are different, and to learn different ways of coping with different people, including total jerks. The first and most important people to learn these lessons from are their parents, even during adolescence. They are learning all the time from both of you, even when you don't realize it. They learn good things that help and bad things that don't help, or even hurt them. Nobody's perfect, so we need to keep learning.

Exercise #11

Before you meet with your coach(s):

Think of something good that your child/ren have learned from you:

____

____

____

Think of something good that you hope to teach your child/ren in the future:

____

____

____

Think of something good that your child/ren have learned from the other parent:

____

____

____

Think of something good that you hope the other parent will teach your child/ren in the future:

____

____

____

Preparing for Joint Session:

Supporting Mom's Role, Supporting Dad's Role

Exercise #12

Before you meet with your coach(es):

Write a way the other parent could support you in teaching your child good skills:

____

____

Write a way that you could support the other parent in teaching your child good skills:

____

____

If your child is resisting contact with one of you, discuss with your coach(es):

Two things you could *say* to help strengthen your child's relationship with the other parent:

1. ____
2. ____

Two things you could *do* to help strengthen your child's relationship with the other parent:

1. ____
2. ____

Write two problems that will arise if there are changes in your child's parenting schedule:

1. ____
2. ____

Write how you can help your child overcome these hurdles:

1. ____
2. ____

JOINT COACHING SESSION

Collaborate with your coach(es) in deciding how to structure this meeting. It is recommended that you start with sharing what you wrote in one or all of the following:

Exercise #10: Proposals for Decisions

Exercise #11: Learning from Mom, Learning from Dad

Exercise #12: Supporting Mom, Supporting Dad

In any of these discussions, remember that you want to work together with moderate behaviors for the benefit of your children.

There is no further structure for the joint session, so that you and the other parent can discuss whatever is appropriate at this stage of your collaborative process. Let the coach(es) guide you in making the best use of this session.

It is important to recognize that this may be a very awkward or easy session, depending on many factors which may be unrelated to these exercises. Therefore, discuss with your coach how you think this session can be structured for the most benefit for both of you and your future communication, decision-making and parenting. If necessary or beneficial, feel free to schedule additional sessions to discuss all of the issues that have been raised here or that you are both ready to discuss.

Preparing for the Child Specialist Meetings

At this point, you have focused on practicing the three conflict-reducing skills of:

Flexible Thinking
Managed Emotions
Moderate Behaviors

There has been a lot of repetition of these skills, so that you will remember them automatically when issues arise. The next step is teaching these skills to your child/ren in meetings with your Child Specialist.

To assist the children and yourself in beginning the Child Specialist Meetings, you may wish to prepare an initial statement to your children at the first Parent-Child session that includes the following issues. An example is in "The New Ways Parent-Child Talk" in Appendix E.

1. New ways in different houses
2. Positive ways with each other
3. Avoiding extreme behaviors
4. Managing our emotions
5. Emotions can be contagious
6. Flexible thinking
7. Rules in both houses

CONGRATULATIONS!

You have completed the Coaching portion of New Ways for Families in Collaborative Divorce

Part II:
New Ways Child Specialist Meetings

Introduction

The overall goal of New Ways for Families is to help both parents develop new ways of communicating, making decisions, and planning for your children in a separation or divorce. New Ways Child Specialist Meetings occur after you have completed New Ways Parent Coaching.

Child Specialist Meetings
You and the other parent will each meet three times with your child/ren with the Child Specialist. You should alternate weeks with the other parent, so that the children hear the same basic messages from each of you, and so each of you hears similar concerns from your children.

In some cases, the Child Specialist and both parents may believe that it is appropriate or preferred that two or all three of these sessions to be joint meetings. In that case, follow the workbook instructions together. However, the way this workbook is written is based on having the first two meetings as each parent separately with the children, then the third meeting as a joint meeting.

Who Meets First?
Which parent meets first with your child/ren can be based on schedules and preferences of the parents. If the child currently favors one parent and resists contact with the other parent, or the child has had no contact with one parent for a while, the first parent to meet with the child should be the "favored" parent. This parent can discuss support for the child meeting with the other parent. Then you should still alternate sessions. Neither parent should have their second session until both parents have had their first session, and the third session should not occur until both have had their second session.

Joint Session

Goals of New Ways Child Specialist Meetings

1. Assist you in teaching your children skills for resilience in the separation or divorce.
2. Assist you in hearing your children's concerns about the separation or divorce.
3. Assist you in discussing new activities and new decision-making for your children.
4. Assist you and the other parent in discussing new ways for your family with the children.

Workbook
Each parent will complete their own Workbook for Part II, just as in Part I. You will use this during the sessions with your child. You will write what your child says in response to certain questions. There is nothing that your child will be expected to write.

Collaborative Family Decision-Making
After you complete New Ways Child Specialist Meetings, the last step is making family decisions for the new ways that your family is organized. This includes:

Your parenting schedule
How to change the parenting schedule
Taking a parenting class separately or together
How you will communicate
How you will jointly make decisions
How you will separately make decisions
How you will plan child activities
How other people (relatives, new partners) are included in your child's lives

Collaborative Divorce is structured to help you and the other parent make these decisions with professional assistance. This will be much easier after you have both practiced the three skills in this workbook and have taught your children the benefits of these skills. That is why you are encouraged to finish New Ways for Families in Collaborative Divorce before you make your big decisions.

New Ways for Families

Child Specialist Meetings

Session 1: Teaching Your Child Skills for Resiliency

The purpose of this first session is to teach your child/ren *flexible thinking*, *managing emotions*, and *moderate behaviors* for resiliency in your separation or divorce. This Workbook and the Child Specialist will help you in these discussions.

Introducing Your Child to Child Specialist Meetings

In the first session of New Ways Child Specialist Meetings, you are the teacher. The Child Specialist is there to help you and your child understand each other, and to assist you as needed in explaining these skills to your child. If you have more than one child, you and the Child Specialist can decide whether to have shorter separate meetings with each child during this session or to meet with them together.

Explain that the Child Specialist is here to help you and your child in discussing difficult issues and learning new skills. Tell your child that you will be meeting with the Child Specialist three times together to talk about New Ways. This is the same Child Specialist who will be meeting with your child and the other parent three times. These skills are so important that they need to learn them from both parents.

Explain to your child that this meeting is about teaching new lessons about life which will help them throughout their lives. These are lessons about dealing with change and about handling close relationships. Tell them that you are going to teach them about *flexible thinking*, *managing emotions*, and *trying new behaviors* for resiliency in your separation or divorce.

Explain that no one is perfect at these things, and that you are going to help them learn these things in the months and years to come. This is just a start. Tell them that you are also learning these new ways and how to use them in your own life, at work, with neighbors, and in your family and friendships.

The New Ways Parent-Child Talk

At this point, give your child a reassuring statement about your positive intentions as you and the other parent organize your family in new ways given the separation or divorce. You can use a statement such as the one in Appendix E at the end of this Workbook. Write the key points you want to make in this statement:

____

____

____

____

____

____

____

Flexible Thinking

Start teaching these skills by explaining flexible thinking to your child. Explain how it is different from all-or-nothing thinking. Explain that when there are a lot of changes people often have all-or-nothing thinking about what will happen, and worry about whether things will be all-good or all-bad. In reality, change is mostly what you make of it.

With flexible thinking, you can both make it better and better as you go along. If one idea doesn't work, you can try another. And if you talk about it together, you can come up with new ideas. Change can bring new opportunities you never had before, and you can learn new things you never knew before.

Tell your child two examples of times when you used flexible thinking in your life and how it was helpful to you. Write them down here:

1. ____

____

2. ____

____

Then, ask your child to give you two examples of how flexible thinking helped somebody they know. If your child can't think of anything, help out by suggesting two shared memories that you and your child both know about. Write them here:

1. ____

____

2. ____

____

If flexible thinking triggers an important good discussion with your children, stay with your discussion. The other two basic skills below can be saved for the beginning of the next session. Otherwise, explain Managing Emotions next.

Managing Emotions

Explain new ways for your children to manage upset emotions. Explain how upset emotions are normal in new situations no matter where you are, who you are, or who you are with. Tell your child how they can *take a break* when they have upset emotions to calm themselves down. Explain how giving themselves *encouraging words* can help them calm down and manage their emotions.

Give an example of a situation in which you had upset emotions and how you were able to calm yourself down. Write the example here:

1. ____

____

Ask your child to describe a situation in which they had upset emotions and how they calmed down their own emotions. Write it down here:

2. ____

____

Practice what you would say to your child when you need to take a break. Practice having your child tell you that they need to take a break to calm down. If there is an important issue to discuss, tell your child it's okay to take a break for a while, as long as you get back together to discuss the important issue. Have each of you practice saying: "I need to take a break for an hour (or a day), then let's talk about this again."

Give your child an example of how you reduced the intensity of your upset emotions so that others were protected from these intense emotions. Write the example here:

1. ____

____

Ask your child for an example of how they managed their upset emotions so that someone else was protected from the intensity of these emotions. Write the example here:

2. ____

____

If your child can't think of an example, try to help them remember a time when you remember that he or she reduced the intensity of their emotions to protect others. Or think of a future situation where it might be a good idea for your child to do this. Write this example above under #2 instead.

[If you are teaching Managing Emotions at the beginning of your second session, skip Moderate Behaviors for now and go to Session 2: Hearing Your Child's Concerns. If necessary, save Moderate Behaviors for your third session with your child.]

Moderate Behaviors

Explain to your child why it is helpful to use moderate behaviors, especially in new situations. Explain how extreme behaviors can make things worse, then you have to spend a lot of time trying to fix the damage of extreme behaviors. Explain how extreme behavior *in response to someone else's extreme behavior* just makes things worse. Give an example of how an extreme behavior got someone you both know into trouble.

Then, tell your child an example of how you used a moderate behavior in a new situation, when you *felt* like using an extreme behavior. Write it here:

1. ____

____

____

____

Then, ask your child for an example of how he or she tried a moderate behavior in a new situation, even when he or she *felt* like using an extreme behavior. Help your child think of an example if he or she cannot. Write the example here:

2. ____

____

____

____

Suggest a new moderate behavior you and your child can try together. Start with something simple, like trying a new board game or going to a new park together. Talk about how it sometimes feels exciting to try something new and other times it feels uncomfortable to try something new. If you and your child have not done a new activity together in a long time, talk about small, moderate steps you might take to accomplish this. Write the new activity here, along with the moderate steps to get started. Discuss the hurdles that might come up to get in the way, and how you can overcome those hurdles.

3. New Activity: ____

____

Step 1: ____

____

Step 2: ____

____

Step 3: ____

____

Step 4: ____

____

Hurdles: ____

____

____

Session 2: Hearing Your Child's Concerns

During this session, the goal is to hear your child's concerns about the separation or divorce. This is an opportunity to use your own skills of *flexible thinking* about what you hear; to *manage your upset emotions*; and to consider *moderate behaviors* after what you have heard (even if you feel like using extreme behaviors).

It is very important that you explain to your child that the focus of this session is for you to just listen and understand. This is not a negotiation session, and it is not a session for changing the parenting schedule or creating a new schedule. It is solely focused on listening and understanding the child's concerns, and answering your child's questions if appropriate.

Your Responses

Some helpful responses to say to your child's concerns may be the following:

Thank you for telling me how you feel.
I can understand how frustrating and upsetting our divorce must be for you.
You are not at all responsible for our separation or divorce.
You are not responsible for my upset feelings—I am, and I am learning to manage them.
I will think about your concerns before we talk at our next meeting
(which will be about trying new ways and moderate behaviors for both of us).

Avoid Questions

Avoid asking your child a lot of specific questions. Leave it up to the child to tell you what is important to him or her. Just say "tell me more" to get them talking more, without directing them. You will get more useful information this way.

However, if you have one question you really want to ask, discuss it with the Child Specialist first. If the Child Specialist believes it is appropriate for this session, he or she will let you know a good time to ask your question.

Managing Your Emotions

Remember to manage your own upset emotions. Expect that your child's concerns may be upsetting to hear, so give yourself some encouraging words. When children tell their parents upsetting information, it means that they trust their parent(s) enough to share all feelings, positive and negative. When children express no negative feelings it means that they do not feel safe, since all children have some negative feelings.

Write down 3 of the most important concerns your child has about the separation or divorce. If you have more than one child, write something about each child's concerns, as they may be different:

1. ____

____

____

____

2. ____

____

____

____

3. ____

____

____

____

Write what you said in response to let your child know you heard his/her concerns:

____

____

____

Session 3 (Joint): Discussing New Ways of Raising Your Child

This session is designed for both parents at the same meeting with the child/ren. If you have made agreements about how you will make decisions, communicate and schedule time with the children, agree on how you are going to present these to the children before this meeting. If you have not made these agreements yet, explain how and when the future decisions will be made.

Before proceeding, you may find it helpful to read the article in Appendix D: Don't Use "Force."

The two goals of this session are:

1. To explain the new ways that you and the other parent are going to make decisions, communicate, and spend time with your child in the new way your family is organized.

2. To discuss having your child try some new, moderate behaviors with each parent.

This can be a fun discussion or a serious discussion, and should be presented in an age-appropriate manner. If it would be beneficial, you can meet with the Child Specialist before meeting with your child/ren.

Decision-making

Inform your child about how decisions are going to be made in the future. Explain which decisions the parents will make jointly, which you will make individually, and which decisions your child can make. If other people will be making some decisions for your family, explain who they are and how they will make these decisions (court, parenting coordinator, etc.).
Write down at least one of each type of decision here:

Parents jointly decide: ____

____

Each parent decides: ____

____

Child can decide: ____

____

Others will decide: ____

____

Discuss any questions your child has about these decisions and think of some examples of each.

Avoid *negotiating* who makes which decisions. Instead, explain and clarify any questions they may have. Children generally want to see that their parents are organized and in agreement, especially in a separation or divorce. Children want to know what the rules are and they usually test their parents until the rules become clear. Expect resistance to your new ways of making decisions and discuss concerns they may have about them. Tell them that you won't always *feel* like making decisions this way, but that you *think* these are good methods and will make a strong effort to stick with them.

Communication

Inform your child about how communication is going to be handled in the future. Explain how the parents will communicate about parenting schedules, changes to the schedule, finances, and activities for the children (email, phone, message book, etc.). Explain how you will communicate in an emergency. Explain how your child can communicate with each of you, such as when your child is at the other parent's house. Explain who your child should talk to about changes in the parenting schedule, money for activities, and complaints about your parenting.

Inform your child of the following methods you and the other parent have already decided. If age appropriate, ask your child what he or she thinks should go in items 4-7 before you fill them in. Only write what you agree are appropriate answers here.

Write down how communication should occur in the future:

1. Parents will usually communicate by: ______________________________

____

2. In an emergency, parents will communicate by: ______________________

____

3. How child should communicate with you from the other parent's house: ________

____

4. Child should talk to you about: ______________________________

____

5. Child should talk to other parent about: ________________________

____

6. Child should complain about you to: ______________________________

____

7. You should complain about child to: ______________________________

____

Avoid *negotiating* these methods of communication, except where appropriate (such as if the child has a good idea to add). If appropriate, make the last two items a fun discussion.

Supporting the Other Parent

Explain to your child how you and the other parent are going to support each other. Give examples of what you are going to say from time to time under each of the following:

Positive comments about each other: ______________________________

____

Repairing statements: ______________________________

____

Following each other's rules: ______________________________

____

Encouraging time with the other parent: ______________________________

____

Explain that if your child doesn't want to visit with the other parent at times, your child is still expected to go and there will be consequences if he or she doesn't go. Say that if there is a need to change the schedule, it needs to be done with the agreement of both parents.

Parenting Schedule

Explain the new parenting schedule to your child. Don't *negotiate* the schedule, except for specific decisions which the child can make. Ask for questions and clarifications of the schedule. Write down key aspects of the schedule here, if you wish:

Trying New Moderate Behaviors

This discussion should focus on ways you can support your child in new activities with yourself and with the other parent. It is helpful to explain to your child that trying new behaviors is often confusing, scary, and we have a natural resistance to change. Yet, new behaviors can also help us learn about life, can help us develop new skills, and help us have new, exciting experiences we didn't know we could have. This is not a negotiation session and not a session for changing the parenting schedule or creating a new schedule. It is focused on *what new behaviors* you will try together, and *how* you will do them. Focus on the specifics and try to make it fun.

Think of new places to eat, fun places to go, new books to read or discuss, new games you might try, something you could build, something you could buy, etc. Ask your child for ideas of new things to do together.

Write down 3 easy new things you can do together that you have never done before:

1. ____

2. ____

3. ____

Write down 3 hard new things you can do together that you have never done before:

1. ____

2. ____

3. ____

Now, jointly pick a realistic new activity you will do together and write down when, where and how you will do it.

New Behaviors with the Other Parent

Discuss with your child activities in the past when they enjoyed being with the other parent. If they cannot think of anything, describe activities you saw them enjoying together.

Write down 3 activities your child/ren previously enjoyed doing with the other parent:

1. ____________________

2. ____________________

3. ____________________

Discuss with your child/ren new realistic activities they can try with the other parent. It is important to present these with a positive tone of voice, as they will pick up any negativity.

Write 3 activities your child/ren can enjoy or learn from while being with the other parent:

1. ____________________

____

2. ____________________

____

3. ____________________

____

Tell or ask your child how you can support him or her doing activities with the other parent. **Write down your child's suggestions.** If your child resists or refuses to do anything with the other parent, explain the importance of your child trying moderate behaviors for his or her own benefit. If necessary, explain what the consequences are if he or she does not make any effort to try to be with the other parent.

Ways you can support your child spending time with the other parent:

____

____

____

Write anything else you want to say to your child at this time:

Finish by saying three things about your child that make you proud and write them here:

CONGRATULATIONS!

YOU HAVE FINISHED NEW WAYS FOR FAMILIES®!

APPENDICES

APPENDIX A

YES, NO, OR I'LL THINK ABOUT IT

By Bill Eddy, LCSW, ESQ.

Whether in a divorce, a workplace dispute, or a conflict with a neighbor, it's easy to get caught up in defending our own behavior and point of view. This is especially true when we are dealing with a high conflict person (HCP). They quickly "push our buttons," and it's easy to react before we know it. They often seem driven to engage in negative conversations rather than trying to solve problems. The focus quickly becomes personal attacks and counter-attacks.

But you don't have to join in. Instead, you can use two simple steps that seem to help, no matter what setting you are in. If you think you are going to be dealing with an HCP, avoid getting hooked and feeding the conflict by reminding yourself of these two steps before you start talking. And if you are in the middle of an argument, you can always shift to this approach.

First, let's look at a couple of typical high conflict arguments in divorce and workplace disputes:

DIVORCE:
Joe [responding to negative feedback]: "So what! Sometimes I have to work late on Fridays, so I'll be late for picking up the kids. You'll just have to live with it if you want me to keep my job. You don't give a s—t about how hard I work to pay you child support!"

Mary: "You are so insulting. I have half a mind to go back to court and just end your visitation. Wait 'til the judge sees all these rude emails you keep sending to me!"

WORKPLACE:
Steve: "You always talk loud in your cubicle next to mine. You are a rude and insensitive person. I don't know why you had to pick this cubicle. It was really pleasant in this office before you moved in!"

Sharon: "You know, you're an a—hole. I have to make a lot more calls than you do. How can you say such B.S. You know you're the busybody here. Nobody likes you. They've all told me, behind your back!"

Instead of getting caught up in these defensive and personal disputes, just focus on two steps:

1) At any point in the dispute, you can say "What do you propose?" Or you can just make a proposal.
2) In response to a proposal, you can simply say: "Yes" "No" or "I'll think about it."
   (If you can both agree to use this approach, you probably are not dealing with an HCP.)

1) First Person: MAKE A PROPOSAL
Whatever has happened before is less important than what to do now. Avoid trying to emphasize how bad the problem is. With a high conflict person, this just triggers more defensiveness.
Plus, people never agree on what happened in the past anyway. Picture a solution and propose it.

For example, in the DIVORCE dispute: "If you're going to be late to pick up the kids on Fridays, then I propose we just change the pickup time to a more realistic time. Instead of 5pm, let's make it 6:30pm."

Or in the WORKPLACE dispute: "I propose that we talk to our manager about finding a better cubicle for you, since you have so many phone calls that need to be made."

2) Second Person: YES, NO, or I'LL THINK ABOUT IT
All you have to do to respond to such a proposal is say: Yes, No, or I'll think about it. You always have the right to say: Yes, No, or I'll think about it. Of course, there are consequences to each choice, but you always have these three choices at least. Here's some examples of each:

YES: "Yes, I agree. Let's do that." And then stop! No need to save face, evaluate the other person's proposal, or give the other person some negative feedback. Just let it go. After all, hostile attacks are not about you. They are about the person making the hostile attack. You are better off to ignore everything else.

NO: "No, I don't want to change the pickup time. I'll try to make other arrangements to get there on time. Let's keep it as is." Just keep it simple. Avoid the urge to defend your decision or criticize the other person's idea. You said no. You're done. Let it drop.

I'LL THINK ABOUT IT: "I don't know about your proposal, but I'll think about it. I'll get back to you tomorrow about your idea. Right now I have to get back to work. Thanks for making a proposal." Once again, just stop the discussion there. Avoid the temptation to discuss it at length, or question the validity of the other person's point of view. It is what it is.

When you say "I'll think about it," you are respecting the other person. It calms people down to know you are taking them seriously enough to think about what they said. This doesn't mean you will agree. It just means you'll think about it.

MAKE A NEW PROPOSAL: After you think about it, you can always make a new proposal. Perhaps you'll think of a new approach that neither of you thought of before. Try it out. You can always propose anything. (But remember there are consequences to each proposal.) And you can always respond: Yes, no, or I'll think about it. (And there are consequences to each of those choices, too.)

AVOID MAKING IT PERSONAL
In the heat of the conflict, it's easy to react and criticize the other person's proposals—or even to criticize the other person personally, such as saying that he or she is arrogant, ignorant, crazy or evil. It's easy and natural to want to say: "You're so stupid it makes me sick." Or: "What are you, crazy?" "Your proposal is the worst idea I have ever heard." But if you want to end the dispute and move on, just ask for a proposal and respond "Yes" "No" or "I'll think about it."

APPENDIX B

Responding To Hostile Mail (B.I.F.F.)

By Bill Eddy, LCSW, ESQ.

Hostile mail – especially email – has become much more common over the past decade. Most of this mail is just "venting," and has little real significance. However, when people are involved in a formal conflict (a divorce, a workplace grievance, a homeowners' association complaint, etc.) there may be more frequent hostile mail. There may be more people involved and it may be exposed to others or in court. Therefore, how you respond to hostile mail may impact your relationships or the outcome of a case.

Do you need to respond?
Much of hostile mail does not need a response. Letters from (ex-) spouses, angry neighbors, irritating co-workers, or attorneys do not usually have legal significance. The letter itself has no power, unless you give it power. Often, it is emotional venting aimed at relieving the writer's anxiety. If you respond with similar emotions and hostility, you will simply escalate things without satisfaction, and just get a new piece of hostile mail back. In most cases, you are better off not responding. However, some letters and emails develop power when copies are filed in a court or complaint process – or simply get sent to other people. In these cases, it may be important to respond to inaccurate statements with accurate statements of fact. If you need to respond, I recommend a B.I.F.F. response: Be Brief, Informative, Friendly and Firm.

BRIEF
Keep your response brief. This will reduce the chances of a prolonged and angry back and forth. The more you write, the more material the other person has to criticize. Keeping it brief signals that you don't wish to get into a dialogue. Just make your response and end your letter. Don't take their statements personally and don't respond with a personal attack. Avoid focusing on comments about the person's character, such as saying he or she is rude, insensitive, or stupid. It just escalates the conflict and keeps it going. You don't have to defend yourself to someone you disagree with. If your friends still like you, you don't have to prove anything to those who don't.

INFORMATIVE
The main reason to respond to hostile mail is to correct inaccurate statements which might be seen by others. "Just the facts" is a good idea. Focus on the accurate statements you want to make, not on the inaccurate statements the other person made. For example: "Just to clear things up, I was out of town on February 12th, so I would not have been the person who was making loud noises that day."

Avoid negative comments. Avoid sarcasm. Avoid threats. Avoid personal remarks about the other's intelligence, ethics or moral behavior. If the other person has a "high conflict personality," you will have no success in reducing the conflict with personal attacks. While most people can ignore personal attacks or might think harder about what you are saying, high conflict people feel they have no choice but to respond in anger – and keep the conflict going. Personal attacks rarely lead to insight or positive change.

FRIENDLY
While you may be tempted to write in anger, you are more likely to achieve your goals by writing in a friendly manner. Consciously thinking about a friendly response will increase your chances of getting a friendly – or neutral – response in return. If your goal is to end the conflict, then being friendly has the greatest likelihood of success. Don't give the other person a reason to get defensive and keep responding.

This does not mean that you have to be overly friendly. Just make it sound a little relaxed and non-antagonistic. If appropriate, say you recognize their concerns. Brief comments that show your empathy and respect will generally calm the other person down, even if only for a short time.

FIRM
In a non-threatening way, clearly tell the other person your information or position on an issue. (For example: "That's all I'm going to say on this issue.") Be careful not to make comments that invite more discussion, unless you are negotiating an issue or want to keep a dialogue going back and forth. Avoid comments that leave an opening, such as: "I hope you will agree with me that ..." This invites the other person to tell you "I *don't agree.*"

Sound confident and don't ask for more information, if you want to end the back-and-forth. A confident-sounding person is less likely to be challenged with further emails. If you get further emails, you can ignore them, if you have already sufficiently addressed the inaccurate information. If you need to respond again, keep it even briefer and do not emotionally engage. In fact, it often helps to just repeat the key information using the same words.

Example
Joe's email: "Jane, I can't believe you are so stupid as to think that I'm going to let you take the children to your boss' birthday party during my parenting time. Have you no memory of the last six conflicts we've had about my parenting time? Or are you having an affair with him? I always knew you would do anything to get ahead! In fact, I remember coming to your office party witnessing you making a total fool of yourself – including flirting with everyone from the CEO down to the mailroom kid! Are you high on something? Haven't you gotten your finances together enough to support yourself yet, without flinging yourself at every Tom, Dick and Harry? ..." [And on and on and on.]

Jane: "Thank you for responding to my request to take the children to my office party. Just to clarify, the party will be from 3-5 on Friday at the office and there will be approximately 30 people there – including several other parents bringing school-age children. There will be no alcohol, as it is a family-oriented firm and there will be family-oriented activities. I think it will be a good experience for them to see me at my workplace. Since you do not agree, then of course I will respect that and withdraw my request, as I recognize it is your parenting time." [And that's the end of her email.]

Comment: Jane kept it brief, and did not engage in defending herself. Since this was just between them, she didn't need to respond. If he sent this email to friends, co-workers or family members (which high conflict people often do), then she would need to respond to the larger group with more information, such as the following:

Jane: "Dear friends and family: As you know, Joe and I had a difficult divorce. He has sent you a private email showing correspondence between us about a parenting schedule matter. I hope you will see this as a private matter and understand that you do not need to respond or get involved in any way. Almost everything he has said is in anger and not at all accurate. If you have any questions for me personally, please feel free to contact me and I will clarify anything I can. I appreciate your friendship and support." [And that's it: B.I.F.F.]

Conclusion

Whether you are at work, at home or elsewhere, a B.I.F.F. response can save you time and emotional anguish. The more people who handle hostile mail in such a manner, the less hostile mail there will be.

APPENDIX C

IS YOUR CHILD "ALIENATED"?

By Bill Eddy, LCSW, ESQ.

IS YOUR CHILD REJECTING ONE PARENT? In divorce or separation, 10% - 15% of children express strong resistance to spending time with one of their parents – and this may be increasing in our society. It may be the father or mother. It may be the parent the child "visits," or the parent where the child lives. Is this the result of abuse by the "rejected" parent? Or is this the result of alienation by the "favored" parent? The idea that one parent can alienate a child against the other has been a big controversy in family courts over the past 20 years, with the conclusion that there are many possible causes for this resistance. Most courts take reports of alienation very seriously and want to know if this is the result of abuse or alienating behavior. Resistance to spending time with a parent is always a serious problem. This needs to be investigated, fully understood, and treated with counseling in many cases. Otherwise, the child's future relationships may be much more difficult.

IS THIS THE RESULT OF ABUSE? The first concern of the courts is protecting the children. If there are reports of child abuse as the cause of the child's alienated behavior, the judge may make a protective order restraining contact with the "rejected" parent, such as a temporary order for supervised visitation. If you are the "rejected" parent you may feel that supervised visitation is unnecessary or insulting. Yet this may be your biggest help, as someone neutral can observe the child's behavior and your relationship. Often the judge will say that he or she will not make any assumptions and wants more information before understanding the cause.

IS THIS THE RESULT OF "PARENTAL ALIENATION SYNDROME?" It is important to know that the courts across the country have not adopted the idea that there is such a syndrome. A syndrome requires a generally accepted cause and effect, and there are many possible causes of children's alienated behavior (abuse by a parent, alienating behavior by a parent, lack of emotional boundaries by a "rejected" parent, lack of emotional boundaries by a "favored" parent, developmental stage, outside influences, etc.). Also, despite alienating behavior by some parents, many children are not resistant to spending time with the other parent. So it is not accepted as a syndrome. However, the courts generally recognize that some children are alienated – they just don't know the reason automatically and often want more information.

WHAT ARE THE SIGNS OF AN ALIENATED CHILD? Children who are not abused, but are alienated have emotionally intense feelings but vague or minor reasons for them. A child might say: "I won't go to see my father!" Yet she might struggle to find a reason: "He doesn't help me with my homework." Or: "He dresses sloppy." Or: "He just makes me angry all the time." Another child might say: "I hate my mother!" Yet again the reasons are vague or superficial: "She's too controlling." "She doesn't understand me like my dad." These children complain that they are afraid of the other parent, yet their behavior shows just the opposite – they feel confident in blaming or rejecting that parent without any fear or remorse. Some of them speak negatively of the "rejected" parent to others, then relax when they are with the "rejected" parent. Others run away, rather than spend time with the rejected parent. All of these behaviors are generally different from those of truly abused children, who are often extra careful not to offend an abusive parent, are often hesitant to disclose abuse and often recant even though it's true.

WHY DO ALIENATED CHILDREN FEEL SO STRONGLY? Alienated children generally show intensely negative emotions and an absence of ambivalence. New research on the brain suggests that this may be the result of the unconscious and nonverbal transfer of negative emotions from parent to child. The parent's intense angry outbursts (even if they are rare), intense sadness, and intensely negative statements about the other parent may be absorbed unconsciously by the child's brain, without the child even realizing it. The child then develops intensely negative emotions toward the other parent (or anyone the upset parent dislikes), but doesn't consciously know why. This may explain the vague or minor reasons given by alienated children for intensely rejecting a good parent. This spilling over of negative emotions from upset parent to child may have begun years before the divorce, so that the child is very tuned in to the upset parent, and automatically and instantly absorbs their emotions and point of view.

DOES CUSTODY MAKE A DIFFERENCE? If one parent has almost all of the parenting time, then the child will not have his or her own experiences with the other parent to know that he or she is not bad. Most states expect children to have substantial time with both parents – except in cases of abuse. Ironically, the amount of time is generally not the biggest factor. The biggest factor is if one parent is constantly spilling over intensely negative emotions to the child about the other parent, while the other parent is following court orders and not addressing these issues at all. For this reason, children can become alienated against either a non-custodial parent or a custodial parent. This can be either the father or the mother. It's like a bad political campaign, with one side campaigning hard and the other side not campaigning at all.

HOW CAN YOU PREVENT ALIENATION? You might be alienating your child against the other parent or against yourself, without even being conscious of it - especially during a divorce. Here are seven suggestions:

1. POSITIVE COMMENTS: Regularly point out positive qualities of the other parent to your child.

2. REPAIRING COMMENTS: All parents make negative comments about the other parent at times. If you realize you made such a comment, follow up with a "repairing comment": "I just spoke negatively about your father [or mother]. I don't really mean to be so negative. He has many positive qualities and I really value your relationship with him. I'm just upset and my feelings are my responsibility, not his and not yours."

3. AVOID REINFORCING NEGATIVE COMMENTS: Healthy children say all kinds of things, positive and negative, about their parents – even about abusive parents. If there is abuse, have it investigated by professionals. If not, be careful that you are not paying undue attention to their negative comments and ignoring their positive comments.

4. TEACH PROBLEM-SOLVING STRATEGIES: If your child complains about the other parent's behavior, unless it is abusive, suggest strategies for coping: "Honey, tell your father something nice before you ask for something difficult." "Show your mother the project you did again, she might have been busy the first time." "If he/she is upset, maybe you can just go to your room and try not to listen and draw a picture instead."

5. AVOID EXCESSIVE INTIMACY: Children naturally become more independent and self-aware as they grow up. Be careful not to be excessively intimate with your child for the child's age, as this may create an unhealthy dependency on you. Examples include having the child regularly sleep with you in your bed beyond infancy; sharing adult information and decisions (such as about the divorce); and excessive sadness at exchanges or how you miss the child when he or she is at the other parent's house.

6. AVOID EXCESSIVE COMPARISONS: When you emphasize a skill or characteristic that you have, don't place it in comparison to weaknesses of the other parent. You each have different skills and qualities that are important to your child. By comparing yourself positively and the other parent negatively (even if this feels innocent), you can inadvertently influence your child. Remember that your child is a combination of both of you, and thinking negatively of one parent means the child may think negatively about half of himself or herself.

7. GET SUPPORT OR COUNSELING FOR YOURSELF: It is impossible to go through a divorce without getting upset some of the time. Protect your child from as much as possible by sharing your upset feelings with adult friends and family, away from your child. Get counseling to cope with the stress you are under.

WILL THE COURT ADDRESS THIS ISSUE? Routinely, in a divorce or separation, the court will order that neither parent shall make disparaging remarks about the other parent within hearing of the child. Some courts may ask you for 3 positive comments about the other parent or 3 steps you are taking to protect the child from absorbing your negative emotions toward the other parent. Think about this seriously, so that you are prepared to answer this question if it is raised. Most of all, practice the suggestions described above.

APPENDIX D

DON'T USE "FORCE"

By Bill Eddy, LCSW, Esq.
©2009 High Conflict Institute

"I won't force the children to go with the other parent," is one of the statements I hear sometimes from parents going through a separation or divorce. This statement has become so common (three times in one day recently), that I decided a short article on this subject would be helpful.

Expectations
Parents have a lot of expectations for their children, for their own benefit. You expect them to go to school. You expect them to do their homework. You expect them to come home at night. You expect them to brush their teeth. You expect them to do their chores. You expect them not to swear in public. You expect them not to have sex. You expect them not to use drugs, etc., etc.

We use all of our resources to "force" them to do (or not do) these things. But we don't use the word "force" with these activities. We use the word "expect." This is a positive word for their long-term benefit, rather than a negative word. And your children get the message. So try not to use the word "force," with all its negativity. Instead, use the positive word "expect." "I expect you to go with your mother/father – we both expect that."

It's Not an Option
Of course, children will resist doing a negative option. They don't want to see the dentist. They don't want to go to school on some days. Even parents don't want to go to work on some days. But most of us go to work anyway, because we need to get paid. It's not an option to stay home.

Somehow, children get the message that going to the other parent's house after a separation or divorce is optional. If you give them a choice and imply it will be a negative experience, any healthy child is going to want to avoid it. Since children have so few options in their lives, if you give them an option to avoid something negative, they will avoid it.

Children Don't Like Moving
Most of the time, children like being where they are. When given a choice, many children who live in two households would rather stay where they are at the moment. It doesn't mean that they don't want to see their Mom or Dad, it just means that they don't want to stop what they're doing, get up, pack up, and go somewhere else. Once they get to the other house, they act just the same way. Don't take it personally: most of the time children just prefer where they are and what they're doing. They live in the present.

Use Positive and Negative Consequences
If children don't do the things that we expect, we usually use consequences with them rather than physically picking them up and taking them. This is especially true with teenagers. Instead, we take away privileges or give new opportunities when they succeed.

Take school, for example. If your child refuses to go to school, do you: Take them out for ice cream? Spend more personal time and attention with them? Take them shopping or to the movies? Allow them to watch TV all day? Surf the internet? If you do, do you think they would increasingly stay away from school? Of course. I have worked with families where this occurred. Instead, if a child resists spending time with the other parent without a very good reason, use the same consequences you would use if they refused to go to school. And don't blame it on the other parent – just be matter-of-fact. In a separation or divorce, attitude is everything.

Avoid Assumptions
In a separation or divorce, it's easy to misinterpret a child's resistance to spending time with one of the parents. It may be about something very minor and the child will change his or her mood soon, unless you give this mood excessive attention or power.

It is easy for a parent to jump to the conclusion that the child has the exact same thoughts about the other parent, such as complicated anger about adult issues that the child may not know about or understand. Or you may be concerned that your child's sadness or anger toward the other parent may mean he or she has been abused or treated badly. While these things could be true, be careful to check them out without making assumptions.

Emotions are Contagious
On the other hand, children do absorb their parent's emotions. It's an important part of how they learn about life, and how they stay connected to their parents. Recent brain research explains how "mirror neurons" cause children to mirror their parents' emotions, as well as behavior. So your child may have picked up your intense emotions about the separation or divorce, and show the exact same fear, sadness, or anger – yet have no logical explanation for it. While it may seem like the child has the same feelings and thoughts that you do, your child may actually just have the same feelings – your feelings.

So be careful not to let your child see or hear your upset feelings about the other parent. Arguments or physical confrontations between parents that are observed by a child can be particularly distressing for a child and may increase their resistance to one parent. Children need to be protected from their parents' behavior sometimes.

Get Family Counseling
If a child develops a resistance to spending time with one parent, it is potentially a serious problem which needs to be treated sooner rather than later. If there is a child abuse issue, it needs to be addressed and stopped. If there has been domestic violence (an incident or a pattern), then this is an important problem to be treated, rather than ignored. Children may be the first to show a problem which needs family attention. And if it is a child absorbing a parent's negative emotions about the separation or divorce, this also needs to get addressed and resolved.

Often the best approach is for a Child Specialist to meet with each parent and the child or children before resistance turns into refusal. And if a child is refusing to see a parent, then it is even more important to take this approach as soon as possible. By meeting with both parents at separate times with the child or children, parents can help and support each other in helping their child. Getting an individual Child Specialist for the child is less effective.

Conclusion
Maybe you can't "force" a child to spend time today with one parent. But you can have consequences, investigate the situation, and get the help of a family counselor. In the long run, it will be better for all of you.

APPENDIX E

THE NEW WAYS PARENT-CHILD TALK

By Bill Eddy, LCSW, ESQ.

When parents separate, having a talk with your children that includes some or all of the following may be helpful (presented in age-appropriate terms). You can say this separately or jointly to your children. It helps if you agree on when you are going to say this to them, and what details you have agreed upon to tell them. For example: parenting schedule, how you will communicate, and how decisions will be made.

1. New ways in different houses: We're going to be organizing our family in new ways from now on. Your mother/father and I are going to be living in different houses and bringing new people into our lives. While we are separating or getting a divorce, we are not separating from you. We will both do everything we can to keep our relationships with you loving and strong. You deserve the best from both of us.

2. Positive ways with each other: We're going to try to act in positive ways with each other. We're going to encourage you to have a strong relationship with both of us. We're going to avoid comparing ourselves to each other, by saying one of your parents is a better person than the other. We both have made mistakes and I am working on myself to be a better person in my life. And we both have strengths that you can learn from, and I will remind you of your mothers'/father's strengths in case you forget occasionally.

3. Avoiding extreme behaviors: As we organize your family in new ways, we are going to try to avoid extreme behaviors by using moderate behaviors, because families are hurt by extreme behaviors. If your mother/father does something extreme, I am still going to try to use moderate behaviors. Because one extreme behavior does not deserve another.

4. Managing our emotions: I am going to try to manage my own emotions as we go through this separation or divorce. You are not responsible for the separation or divorce, and you are not responsible for my feelings. I alone am responsible for how I manage my emotions and for protecting you from my most intense emotions. This will be a hard time and I will not be perfect.

5. Emotions can be contagious: I understand that emotions can be contagious, so I will try to reassure you that you do not have to have my emotions. You are a separate person and will have your own emotions about this separation or divorce. You should always feel free to talk about your feelings with me and I will respect your feelings, even when they are different from mine. The most important thing is that I will try to do my best to let you continue to be a child while I continue to be a parent.

6. Flexible thinking: I am going to use flexible thinking in handling our separation or divorce. This means that you can approach me with any ideas about what you and I can do together, and about the new ways our family will be operating. But remember that your mother/father and I will be doing the decision-making. This means I will try to solve problems without getting

stuck in all-or-nothing thinking where I only see one solution. There are many ways to make our lives work well together and I will be open-minded.

7. Rules in both houses: There will still be rules in each of our houses, even though some of the rules will be different. We both expect you to follow the other parent's rules when you are in the other's house.

Do you have any questions about these new ways of doing things?

www.ingramcontent.com/pod-product-compliance
Lightning Source LLC
Jackson TN
JSHW060922050126
96225JS00006B/8